First published 1974
Reprinted 1976, 1977, 1979
Macdonald Educational
Holywell House
Worship Street
London EC2A 2EN

© Macdonald Educational
Limited, 1974

ISBN 0 356 04888 8
(Cased edition)
ISBN 0 356 06501 4
(Limp edition)

Made and printed by
Purnell & Sons Ltd
Paulton, Avon,
England

**Editor**
Verity Weston

**Design**
Sarah Tyzack

**Production**
Philip Hughes

**Illustrators**
Peter Connolly
Anne Mieke
Colin Rose
Peter North/The Garden
    Studio
Richard Hook/Temple Art
Maggie Heslop/Fred and
    Jo Thompson
John Smith
Peter Thornley
Ron Hayward Associates
Pat Ludlow/Freelance
    Presentations
Eric Jewell

**Consultant**
Harry Strongman
Senior Lecturer in History,
Berkshire College of
Education

**Photographs**
National Tourist Organisation of Greece: 49(T)
Spectrum: 10, 15
Sonia Halliday: 43(T), 45, 49 (B)
Mansell Collection: 13(B), 44
National Museum of Athens: 43
Peter Connolly: 36, 37
George Rainbird: 13(T)

Fitzwilliam Museum, Cambridge: 17(T)
Museum of Classical Archaeology, Cambridge: 17(B)
Phaidon Press: 20, 22
Michael Holford: 35(B), 38, 39, 47
Picturepoint: 12, 32
Pictor: 30
Royal Ontario Museum, Toronto: 40
Science Museum, London (Crown Copyright): 34

# The Greeks

**Judith Crosher**

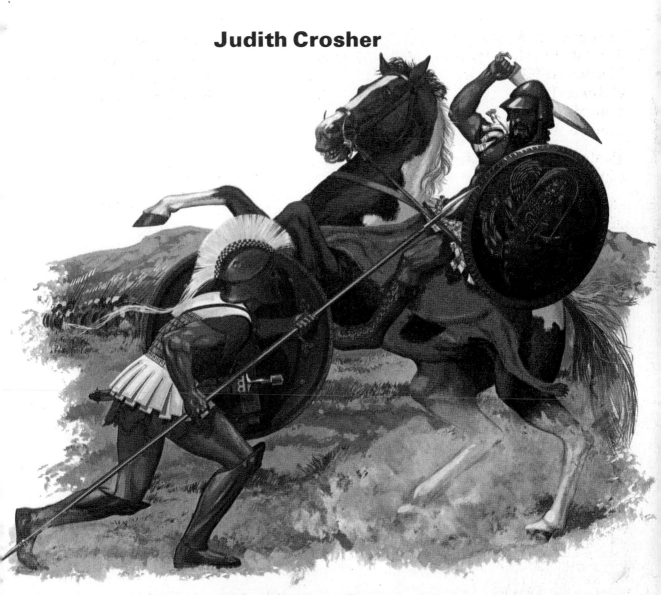

**Macdonald Educational**

# The Greeks

Between 1500 and 1200 BC the Mycenean civilization developed in Greece, with kings such as Agamemnon ruling from magnificent palaces. From 1200 BC this civilization gradually collapsed when tribes from Central Europe invaded Greece and other Mediterranean countries.

The palaces were deserted and the people turned back to simple farming. Even the art of writing was forgotten. The Mycenean civilization became only a memory, handed down in stories from parents to children.

Between 1100 and 500 BC, a new civilization grew up. Groups of villages gradually organized themselves into tiny, independent states, known as city-states.

Our ideas about government, science, mathematics, medicine, history, philosophy, art, architecture and theatre owe much to the Greeks who lived in city-states between about 500 and 400 BC. These were the years that are now known as the Age of Classical Greece.

This book describes the life of the Greek people at home, at work and at war during those years. It concentrates mainly on Athens. This is partly because we know most about Athens and partly because Athens had an important influence on many other city-states.

There are several ways of finding out about the people who lived in Greece over 2000 years ago. There are the writings of people living at the time. There are ancient buildings, some well-preserved and some in crumbled ruins. And there are the objects found in archaeological sites, such as tools, carvings and pottery.

All the information in the text and illustrations comes from these sources. Together they tell us what it was like to be a Greek living in Classical Greece.

# Contents

# The agora

In 500 BC a Greek lived in a very small independent state consisting of a town and the farmland around it. He called this a city-state. At the centre of the town there was an open space called the *agora*. The word *agora* once meant a meeting. The Greeks started to use this word for their town centre because the men met there to discuss the important matters of the city-state.

The *agora* was the busy heart of the life of the city-state. In many cities, all the citizens met there at an assembly to decide how to run their state. The city judges tried people there. Men strolled with their friends in the shady arcades. And every year all the people of the city met in the *agora* to watch the festivals of poetry and games held in honour of the gods.

In the picture below, you can see the hustle and bustle of the daily market which was held around the edge of the Athens *agora*. The men did the shopping. The Greeks had no shopping bags, so a soldier carries his fish in his helmet. One man visits the barber while another buys some sandals. The slave-trader tries to persuade a customer to buy two newly-captured, strong slaves. And in a quiet, cool spot under the trees, a group of friends discuss politics and the latest gossip.

▼ The *agora* at Athens in the fifth century BC. Historians know what it must have been like from studying the archaeological remains and from descriptions written at the time.

# Growth of a city-state

A Greek thought of himself, not as part of a nation, but as a member of a city-state. In 500 BC Greece was divided into many tiny, independent states. The smallest state was only a few miles wide. The largest, Attica, took two days to walk across. On the next page you can see how the city-states grew up.

In about 800 BC aristocrats usually ruled each small town. But as the town grew, traders became richer and wanted a share in government. The farmers too wanted changes. As the population grew, land became scarce. Many farmers had to emigrate, others fell into debt and some even had to sell themselves as slaves.

Between 700 and 600 BC there were revolutions in some states and the people helped tyrants to seize power. In other states, a chief magistrate, or public official, was chosen to make new laws. Gradually, the right to share in governing was given to more people. By 500 BC male citizens with a certain amount of property could vote in some states. In others, all male citizens had this right.

▲ *Monarchy.* The king rules alone or with a council of nobles. He is chief priest, leads the army and deals out justice.

▲ *Tyranny.* Rule by a man who takes power by force. He was often supported by the people against harsh aristocrats.

▲ Greece is divided into valleys by rocky ranges. This may ...tly explain why small, independent states developed.

▲ *Democracy.* All male citizens share in law-making. Women, children and slaves were not counted as citizens.

# ► How the city-state grew 900-600 BC

## Methods of government

▲ *Aristocracy.* The nobles take over the king's powers and govern. When they die, their sons take their place.

▲ *Oligarchy.* Rule by a few, usually those with a certain amount of property. Athenians called it "Rule of the fat".

The villagers in a valley build a fortress, called a *polis,* on a central hill. When an enemy invades, they and their animals take shelter behind its wooden walls.

Gradually, people leave their villages and settle near the safe fortress wall. The village nobles come and govern the settlement which becomes the main town.

By 600 BC, most people in the area have moved there. A second wall is built. The word *polis* now means the city and the land around it, that is, the city-state.

# Citizens of Athens

By the fifth century BC, all the citizens of city-states such as Athens took a share in governing their state. This sounds rather like a modern democracy. But our states are so big that we elect representatives to debate and vote for us. The Athenians did not only decide how to run their state. They actually shared directly in running it.

Every year, nearly a fifth of the 40,000 adult male citizens of Athens took their turn as judges, public officials and council members. Every official did his job for one year. A man could be a general one year and an ordinary soldier the next.

▼ You can see that the old walls round the Acropolis in Athens are still there. The word *acropolis* means a high fortress. Most city-states had an *acropolis*, once called a *polis*, on a hill in the middle of the city.

Nearly all the state jobs were part time. Most citizens had their own farms or workshops so they could take time off when they needed it. This method of government only worked because people felt that helping to run the state was as important as their own work. They thought that anyone who was not interested in state affairs was stupid.

Everyone could be a councillor, a judge or an official at least once. Even when he was not serving as an official, an Athenian took part in government through the assembly. The assembly, where all the citizens met each month, really ran the state. Everyone knew how to do each state job because all the jobs were discussed in the assembly. And the generals and officials could not go to war, raise taxes, change laws or spend state money without asking the assembly.

## Government jobs done by Athenian citizens

▲ 500 councillors were chosen by lot. They prepared items for the assembly to discuss and they supervised the officials.

▲ 6000 judges were chosen by lot. They sat on juries to hear and judge quarrels between citizens.

When a judge was chosen to serve for a year, a bronze ticket with his name was put into the slab above. Every day lots were drawn to choose the rows of names to serve.

The judges sat in groups of 301 to 1001 to hear cases. There were no lawyers. The citizens spoke for themselves.

Sometimes citizens paid writers to make up speeches for them. A man might also bring his children to court in rags to get the judges' sympathy.

▲ Officials included ten generals, ten *archons* chosen by lot to run festivals and administer laws, and about 1000 other officials.

# Sparta's soldier-citizens

▼ All the Spartans lived in five towns. The *helots* worked the farmland. The *perioeci*, freemen without votes, lived in the villages. They provided the other goods the Spartans needed. In the diagram one figure equals about 12,000 people.

◆ Spartan towns

◆ Helots' dwellings

◆ Perioeci villages

Life in many Greek city-states was similar to that in Athens. But the people in one city-state, Sparta, lived very differently.

The Spartans had invaded the region of Laconia in Greece in the twelfth century BC. They took over the farmers' land but made the farmers stay there as *helots,* or slaves. These *helots* had to give half their produce to the Spartans. And the whole Spartan way of life was aimed at controlling their huge slave population.

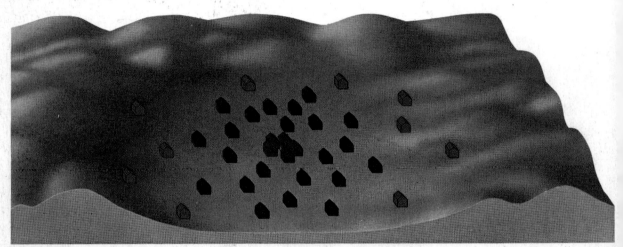

Perioeci    Helots    Spartan    Helots    Perioeci

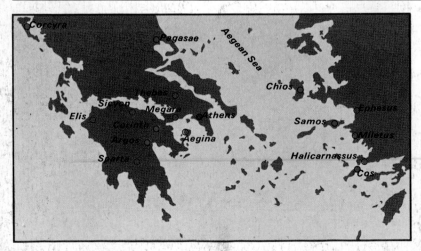

● *Over 100,000 inhabitants*

● *65,000-100,000 inhabitants*

● *30,000-65,000 inhabitants*

◀ The map shows Athens and Sparta and some of the largest Greek city-states. But most city-states had fewer than 10,000 people.

The city-states on the Aegean islands and in Asia were founded by Greeks in the twelfth century BC.

Every Spartan citizen was a full-time soldier who spent his life training in case the *helots* rebelled. At seven, a Spartan boy left his mother and went to live in a camp in the mountains. Here, barefoot and in a thin tunic in all weathers, he exercised, played war games and learned the state laws. Even when he grew up, he still lived in a barracks and visited his wife secretly. For two years he would be in the secret police which searched out and killed troublesome *helots*.

A Spartan girl also had to do hard physical training so that she would bear strong children. The Spartans despised comfort, good food, soft clothes, useless talk and new ideas, and they had no art.

▼ A statue of the famous Spartan king, Leonidas, stands at the Pass of Thermopylae. With 300 Spartans, he held the pass for two days against the whole Persian army until every Spartan was killed. There is more about the wars against the Persians on page 53.

# Houses in the city

▲ The front of a house as it would have looked from the street. Some houses probably had an upper storey at the back.

Up on the *acropolis* and in the *agora*, the public buildings and temples were of brightly-painted marble. But the houses in the dirty, twisting streets were mostly built of sun-dried mud bricks. There were no splendid mansions. Even a great general like Themistocles lived in a plain villa just like his next door neighbours. Rich men were not respected for the amount that they spent on themselves, but for what they gave to the gods and to the city to pay for the public festivals.

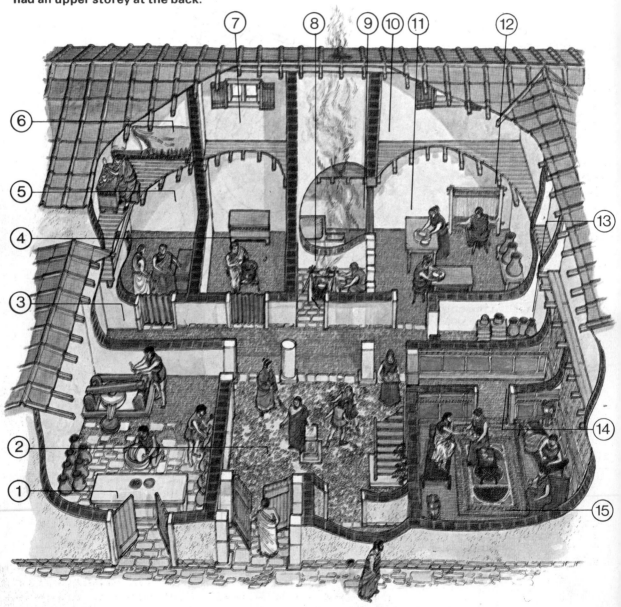

Only the larger houses had stone floors. In others, the walls were built straight up from the flattened earth. The mud-brick walls were so soft that burglars were called "wall-breakers". They simply dug their way in.

Archaeologists have found tools on the floors of rooms next to streets. This probably means that a craftsman often used the room next to the street as his workshop.

The other rooms opened on to a central courtyard and few windows faced the street. This was because in larger cities an open drain ran down the middle of the street. The hole in the bathroom led to this drain. Smaller cities had no drains at all. All the rubbish was thrown into the street, to be picked over by dogs.

▲ Many houses had no bathrooms. This painting on a Greek vase shows a boy washing in a large pot.

Archaeologists can tell us about richer people's houses from the stone remains they find. There are no remains of poorer people's houses, for they were made entirely of mud bricks and have crumbled away.

◄ In 430 BC a new suburb was laid out in Olynthus in North Greece. From the stone foundations and mosaic floors found there, the artist has reconstructed this picture of what a comfortable family home must have looked like.

1. Men press olives in the shop.
2. An altar stands in the open courtyard. The porter's lodge is on the right of the entrance.
3. The covered portico.
4 and 5. The living rooms are heated by charcoal braziers.
6 and 7. The women's bedrooms.
8. Smoke from the open fire rises straight to the roof.
9. Bathroom with a pottery tub.
10. The women's sitting room.
11 and 12. Women grind corn and weave cloth in the kitchen.
13. Store room or slaves' room.
14. Ante-room.
15. Couches stand on a raised ledge around the men's dining room. Unwanted food is thrown onto the floor. A drain in the floor leads to the street.

▲ The girl on this carving, or relief, is ready to wash. There was no soap. People rubbed olive oil on their skin, scraped it off and splashed themselves with water.

# Inside the house

Even a rich man's house, like the one on page 16, would seem rather uncomfortable to us. There were no carpets on the floors and no glass in the windows. In winter, the air would be smoky from the fires of charcoal braziers and oil lamps.

The ancient Greek houses have crumbled and the wood and leather furniture rotted away long ago. We can only tell what rooms looked like from paintings on pottery vases and from reliefs. It seems that there were no shelves or cupboards. Everything, from cups to musical instruments, was hung from nails in the wall. Blankets were stored in chests, and the couches were made up as beds each night. Slaves probably slept on the kitchen floor.

▼ At dinner, men lay on couches while women sat on stools or chairs. A slave brought in the food for each person on a small table. These tables were low enough to be pushed under the couches when they were not being used.

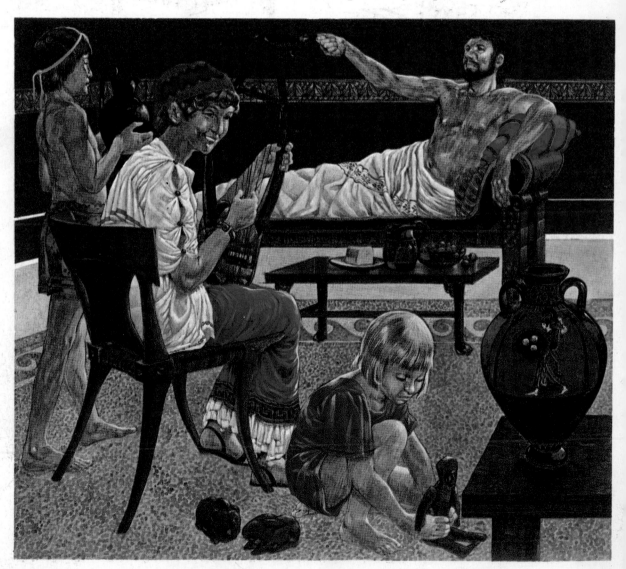

These pieces of furniture are "reconstructions". Modern craftsmen have made them, copying the furniture shown on Greek vase paintings.

► The Greeks loved to paint scenes of home life, like this one, on their vases.

▼ This pottery high-chair was found in Athens. It proves that the painter made his picture true to life.

# Life at home

"I never spend my time indoors: my wife is quite able to manage the household by herself," says a character in Xenophon's book *Oeconomicus*. This was the rule in all families. After a snack at dawn, the man went out until nightfall. He did the shopping, worked in his workshop and did some work as a juryman or council member. He also spent a lot of time talking with his friends about new ideas, politics or just gossip.

Apart from visiting her friends and going to the city festivals, a Greek wife stayed out of sight at home. But this did not mean that she was lonely or had nothing to do. She had her relations, slaves, children and neighbours for company. She had to organize all the household work. This included spinning and weaving, taking care of the stores, fetching water from a public fountain and filling the oil lamps. The pictures on the right give more information about a Greek woman's life.

Unwanted babies, especially girls, were put out in pots to die in the fields or streets.

Xenophon says a wife's duties are: to manage the money and to oversee the weaving;

◄ The wife keeps blankets, her spare clothes and her husband's armour in this chest. Her work basket, mirror, oil jug and cup hang on the wall.

► Children's toys were made of clay, leather or beeswax. The clay doll, about 152 mm. (6 in.) high, was once brightly painted. When children died, their toys were buried with them to keep them company in the underworld.

Although girls did not go to school, an educated house-slave might teach them to read.

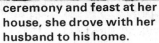

At 15, a girl gave away her toys and married the man chosen by her father. After a private ceremony and feast at her house, she drove with her husband to his home.

to keep the wine cool and the corn dry and to teach new slaves their duties.

There were no full-time soldiers. When his turn came, her husband went off to war.

Every morning the housewife made a small offering to the gods protecting the household.

# Cooking and eating

We know what people liked to eat from the poetry written about food. No food is more often mentioned than fish, and no-one is more hated than the fishmonger. "That villainous man," according to the poet Antiphanes, is rude to his customers, charges too much and only smiles when he is trying to get rid of rotten fish.

Butchers are never mentioned in poetry, for there were none. People seldom ate meat except at religious festivals. Then, the goat or lamb would be taken home alive to be sacrificed in the courtyard. The entrails and fat were burnt on the altar as an offering to the gods. The rest of the meat was roasted by a special meatcook hired from the market for the occasion. Cows were kept for the big city festivals and, after the sacrifice, the meat was shared among the poor.

The evening dinner was the only hot meal of the day. It was usually served in two courses, with fish and vegetables in the first, followed by cheese, cakes, radishes and dried fruit. The Greeks ate a great deal of bread, for there were no potatoes or rice. They used honey for sweetening. Some of the dishes, such as brains or thrushes in honey, might seem strange to us now.

*Drinking bowl*

*Drinking cup*

*Wine jug*

*Mixing krater*

*Drinking cup*

*Wine cooler*

▲ Wine was mixed with water in a *krater* before being served. Each drinker began by pouring a drop on the ground as an offering to the gods.

► This vase painting shows Greek men at dinner. Dinner parties were for men only. They discussed politics, made up poems and riddles and sang rounds. They ate food such as that on the menu below.

**DINNER PARTY MENU**

*Cutlet of eel*

*Squid*

*Slice of black pudding*

*Boiled pig's trotters*

*Ribs of pork*

*Small wild birds*

*Cheese in honey*

Slavewomen prepare supper in the kitchen. All the grain had to be ground by hand at home.

Everyone rose at dawn and ate a simple breakfast of bread dipped in diluted wine. Lunch was mainly bread with a piece of goatsmilk cheese or some olives and figs.

A peasant's supper consisted of barley porridge and barley bread. There might also be vegetables stewed in olive oil, and a jay or swallow trapped in the fields.

In wealthier homes, dinner was basically the same but the bread was made of wheat. Extra dishes of fish, sausage, cheese in honey, and nuts were also served.

# A potter's workshop

A Greek citizen thought that the only decent way of making a living was to farm your own land or to be a craftsman such as a stonemason, a potter or a metalworker. The idea of working for someone else was almost like slavery.

Even the state had no permanent workers apart from its slave clerks. When men were needed to build a temple, the city gave out hundreds of small jobs to the craftsmen. Helped by his slaves, a craftsman would carve a column or cart a load of marble and then go back to his workshop.

The potter was a very important craftsman. Almost all household goods, from lamps and cooking pots to tiles and toys, were made of clay. The potter worked in his workshop helped by slaves and apprentices, and customers would come to the workshop to order their goods. The black glaze of Athenian pots was admired all over the ancient world and Athens exported pottery throughout the Mediterranean.

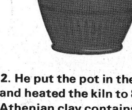

We have only just discovered how the shiny black glaze on Athenian pots was made.
1. The potter mixed fine clay with water. The mixture became a brown jelly with which he painted his design.

2. He put the pot in the kiln and heated the kiln to 800°C. Athenian clay contains a lot of iron. The iron in the clay absorbed oxygen from the air which turned the whole pot a reddish colour.

3. He closed the air vent at the top of the kiln and made the kiln steamy. He raised the temperature to 945°C. The oxygen was forced out of the iron and the whole pot turned black.

4. When he opened the vent again, oxygen rushed in. The parts which had not been painted turned red again. But the jelly-like paint was too thick to absorb oxygen and the painted parts stayed black.

In this potter's workshop, one man paints a vase, while another makes a pot on his wheel. Outside, a slave is about to load the kiln with finished pots which now need firing.

# Clothes and fashions

In every home, from the richest to the poorest, it was the women's job to make the cloth for tunics, cloaks and blankets. A sheep's fleece was bought whole in the market and washed in the courtyard at home. After the burrs had been picked out and the fleece had been beaten into hanks, it was ready for dyeing, spinning and weaving. The strip of woven material from the loom was ready to wear. There was no need for cutting and sewing.

▲ In winter and when they were travelling, men wore felt hats and soft leather boots.

▲ To make men look more noble, sculptors often showed them draped only in long cloaks.

▶ This lady has woven a scarf to match her tunic on a small hand-loom.

The convenient thing about Greek clothes was that you could get dressed so quickly. You had no underclothes, just a piece of cloth pinned and tied to make a tunic called a *chiton*. Another piece was draped over it as a cloak. Young men and slaves wore short *chitons*; women and older men wore long ones. The *chitons* had no pockets; Greeks carried money tucked in their cheeks.

Looking at statues, we imagine that everyone wore white. In fact women loved brightly-dyed clothes. A man might wear a plain white tunic with a narrow coloured border in the daytime, but his evening clothes were often red, brown, green, indigo or yellow ochre.

▲ Hairstyles shown on sculptures. By the fifth century BC most men wore their hair short.

▲ A comb and mirror. Women painted their eyes with soot and their cheeks with mulberry juice.

▲ Jewellery was mainly made of gold, and set with coral, agate, amber and cornelians.

**Putting on a *chiton***

*Method one.* Fold the cloth twice and pin it at the shoulders. Tie the belt over or under the flap of cloth.

*Method two.* Fold the cloth and pin along the top. Tie in two places and pull out the cloth between the belts.

# A slave's life

▼ We cannot be sure what the population of Athens was, but historians have made estimates. Each figure equals 5000 people.

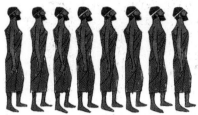

▲ 40,000 adult male citizens. Most had a wife and children.

▲ 35,000 men slaves worked on farms or in small workshops.

▲ 25,000 women slaves helped with housework and children.

▲ 10,000 child slaves training for a craft or housework.

▲ 20,000 mine-slaves dug the silver discovered in 483 BC.

Even in democratic states, most people had no share in governing the city. Women, foreigners and slaves were not thought of as citizens and therefore could not vote. Even when a slave was set free, he could own a shop or serve in the army, but not become a citizen.

Athens and many other city-states had huge populations of slaves. Anyone could become a slave. You could be kidnapped by pirates at sea or captured in war.

Slaves who lived with a family were usually well-treated and often loved. They were expected to be faithful and were tortured before speaking in a court because otherwise they might hide facts which could hurt their masters.

A slave had to work for whoever bought him, unless his friends sent him money to buy back his freedom. He could also save up to buy his freedom or be set free when his master died.

But the slaves who mined the silver that made Athens rich had no hope of freedom. Branded, and chained together, they worked long shifts in small underground tunnels until they died of exhaustion.

▼ A citizen earned about 15 *drachmae* a month. He and his slave could each earn a *drachma* a day on public work. He might let the slave keep one-sixth.

Skilled technician 6000

Craftsman 300

Attractive girl 300

Mine-slave 150

Male house-slave 166

166

Child slave 72

Lydian woman 170

▶ Prices of slaves compared with other goods. The prices are in *drachmae*. Most families had only a girl for the house and a man for the workshop or farm.

Couch 17

Linen curtain 11

Table 4

◀ At the Athens music school, slave-girls were trained as singers and dancers and hired out to entertain at parties.

▶ A slave-girl holds the head of a young man who has had too much to eat and drink at a party. Sometimes men fell in love with and married slave dancing girls. But a slave-girl's sons could not be citizens.

# The farmer's year

Even in the fifth century BC, most people were farmers. For many, life was very hard. Each farm was only about two hectares (five acres). This was enough to support a small family. But the soil was poor and land was scarce. When the population grew, many people were forced to emigrate to find new land.

We can get an idea of the difficulties and struggles of a farmer's life from a poem called *Works and Days*. This was written by Hesiod in about 700 BC.

If you want to prosper, Hesiod says, keep working even in winter. Do not marry early. Have only one son because you will not be able to support more. Sacrifice regularly to the gods. Remember the lucky days for each job and avoid the unlucky ones. Otherwise your animals will fall sick and your corn will rot.

Be friendly with your neighbours because they are near if you need help. Besides, with a bad neighbour, you never know what will happen to your ox. Try not to borrow, never lend anything, and do not trust anyone.

▲ A farmer's life in ancient Greece was quite similar to the life of this Greek peasant today. The ancient Greeks kept donkeys and goats too. They farmed the same countryside and also made terraces on the hills for their vines.

**Gamelion (January-February)**

The farmer prunes his grape-vines and cleans and mends his tools.

**Thargelion (May-June)**

The farmer relaxes in the shade while the hired man mends the barns.

**Boedromion (September-October)**

The ground under the trees is swept and the olives are shaken down.

## Anthesterion
### (February-March)

...ploughs the fallow ...ld and leaves it bare ...til November.

## Elaphebolion
### (March-April)

He tends the vines, picking off caterpillars and pulling out weeds.

## Munychion
### (April-May)

A hired man helps to harvest the wheat. This field will now lie fallow.

## Skirophorion
### (June-July)

...e farmer threshes the ...heat to separate the ...ain from the chaff.

## Hecatombaion
### (July-August)

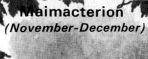

The grain and cheese are taken to market by mule or by boat.

## Metageitnion
### (August-September)

The grapes are picked, spread out in the sun for ten days, and pressed.

## Pyanopsion
### (October-November)

...e farmer ploughs the ...allow land again and ...ows wheat or barley.

## Maimacterion
### (November-December)

The women spin and weave the wool for blankets and tunics.

## Poseidaion
### (December-January)

On cold winter days, the men meet to chat in the warm blacksmith's shop.

# Greeks abroad

▲ A coin from Syracuse. Before coins were invented, trade was done by the exchange of goods.

The people who emigrated from Greece in the seventh and eighth centuries BC went because they were starving at home. The population in each city-state was growing and there was not enough land to go around. Each city solved this problem by finding empty land around the Mediterranean or Black Sea. Then the city collected together its landless families and sent them off with a supply of food and seed. Each group shared the land out and set up a new, independent city-state.

▲ Temples such as this one at Agrigento in Sicily mark the places where Greek colonies were founded. Earth and fire from the homeland were kept inside the temples.

**Exported from Etruria**

Iron

Copper

Slaves

Hemeroscopion

The map shows the Greek colonies and their exports to Greece. The cities shown by purple dots were the chief founders of colonies abroad. Most of the grain went to Athens, and she exported silver, pottery, olive oil and wine.

Over the years, trade grew up between the new city-states abroad and the old ones at home. Trading between the colonies and mainland Greece could be profitable, but it was also risky. A ship might be attacked by pirates or an enemy state, or wrecked in a storm.

There were no large shipping companies. Each trader sailed his own ship. Groups of men clubbed together to buy a cargo to export. They then waited anxiously for months to see if they had made or lost a fortune.

The trader sailed all summer, buying and selling at each port. He changed course when he heard of a likely market or a good harvest. In autumn he returned with his cargo of grain, tame apes, timber and slaves.

▼ **Another coin from Sicily. Each Greek city-state issued its own coins.**

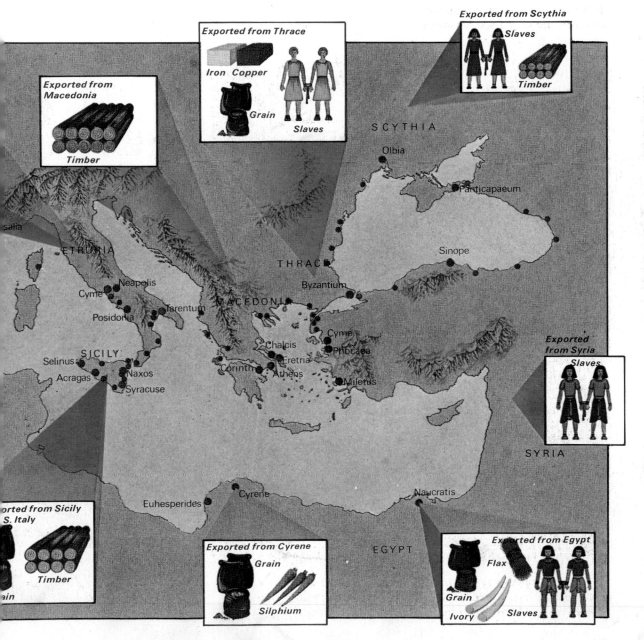

**Exported from Scythia**
Slaves
Timber

**Exported from Thrace**
Iron  Copper
Grain
Slaves

**Exported from Macedonia**
Timber

**Exported from Syria**
Slaves

**Exported from Sicily & S. Italy**
Timber
Grain

**Exported from Cyrene**
Grain
Silphium

**Exported from Egypt**
Flax
Grain
Ivory
Slaves

SCYTHIA
Olbia
Panticapaeum
Sinope
THRACE
Byzantium
MACEDONIA
Cyme
Phocaea
Chalcis
Eretria
Corinth
Athens
Miletus
ETRURIA
...salia
Neapolis
Cyme
Posidonia
Tarentum
SICILY
Selinus
Acragas
Naxos
Syracuse
Cyrene
Euhesperides
Naucratis
SYRIA
EGYPT

# Merchant ships and warships

▶ A model of a Greek *trireme*. A *trireme* was about 35 m. (115 ft.) long and 5 m. (16 ft.) wide.

It could ram the enemy with its prow. Or the oarsmen could get up speed, pull in their oars and sweep past the enemy ship, breaking off its oars.

The *trireme* carried 170 oarsmen, ten officers, two archers, 14 foot-soldiers and the commander.

Leather thongs fastened the sails to the mast.

The hull was made of fir for lightness.

The painted eye was either to keep off evil spirits or for the ship to "see" where it was going.

The ram was made of bronze.

Bow

The roads in ancient Greece were so bad that you often could not tell a road from a dried-up riverbed. So it was much easier and quicker to travel by sea.

A Greek trader's merchant ship was made of oak and was solid and squat. It had a large hull for all the cargo. The ship was too heavy to row far and so depended on its sails. A trader therefore sailed near the coast in case the wind dropped or a squall blew up.

During the fifth century BC the heavy, slow merchant ships were often protected by light, fast warships called *triremes*. Athens was the main naval power. City-states who were friendly with Athens paid towards her navy. In return, she protected them against invaders and their ships against pirates.

Athens built the *triremes* and paid the crews. Each year she chose 400 rich citizens. Each citizen had to keep one ship in good order. If he wanted to, the citizen could command his *trireme* at sea for that year.

A thick rope ran under the keel of the ship. It was fastened on deck at bow and stern. When it got wet, it tightened, helping to keep the ship's timbers in place.

There were three rows of oars. The bottom two rows came through the portholes. The top row rested on a wooden framework sticking out from the side of the ship.

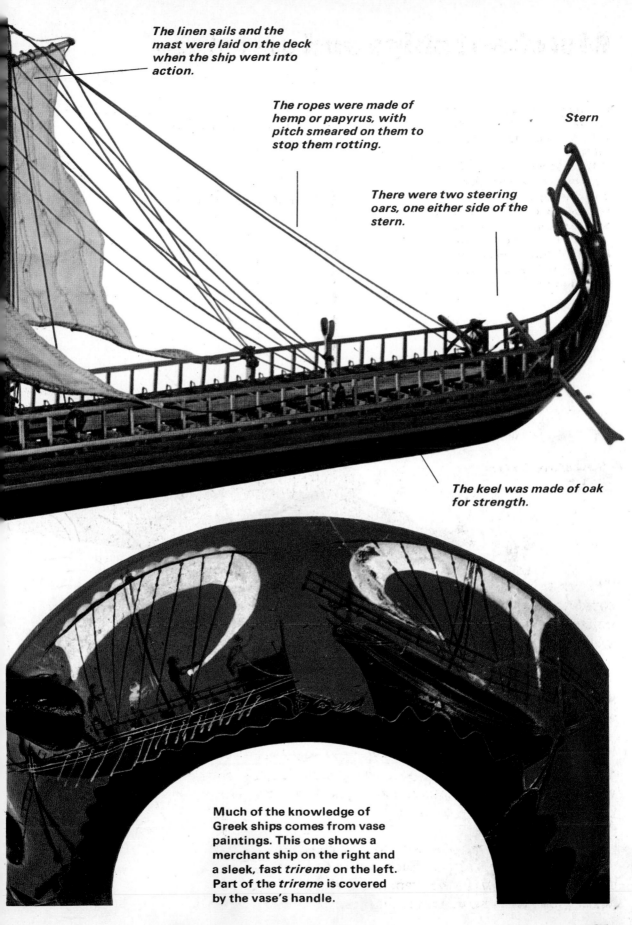

The linen sails and the mast were laid on the deck when the ship went into action.

The ropes were made of hemp or papyrus, with pitch smeared on them to stop them rotting.

Stern

There were two steering oars, one either side of the stern.

The keel was made of oak for strength.

Much of the knowledge of Greek ships comes from vase paintings. This one shows a merchant ship on the right and a sleek, fast *trireme* on the left. Part of the *trireme* is covered by the vase's handle.

# Battles and soldiers

There were no full-time professional soldiers in the fifth century. Every citizen could be called up at any time until he was sixty. In Athens, all 18-year-olds did two years' military service, one in the garrison at the naval port of Munychia and one in a border fort. After the first year, each recruit was given a sword and shield embossed with the state's emblem.

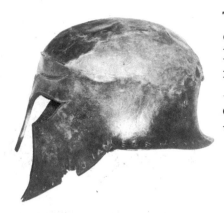

▲ A *hoplite's* bronze helmet had a horsehair plume. His bronze shield was lined with linen or leather.

▲ If a *hoplite* wore foot-armour, it was riveted to his sandal. His breastplate was of stiffened linen covered with bronze plates.

▶ A fight between a *hoplite* and a cavalry-man.

Every spring, a citizen went to the *agora* to see if his name was up for service that year. If it was, he had to be ready to go to war at a day's notice. The kind of soldier he became depended on what armour he could afford. The poor fought with hunting slings and bows, or rowed the warships. Horses were for the rich.

However, fighting from horseback was not very efficient. A horseman had no saddle or stirrups. He had to keep his balance with his knees, so could not deliver very heavy blows. The *hoplites*, foot-soldiers with lances and double-edged swords, were an army's best fighters.

▲ A cavalry-man's helmet. Because he needed one hand for the reins, he often did not carry a shield.

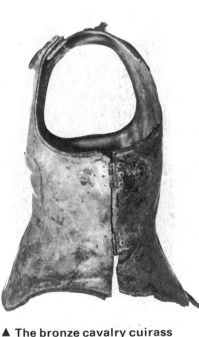

▲ The bronze cavalry cuirass was hinged at the side. It curved out at the bottom so that the rider could sit comfortably.

# A city goes to war

▲ Greek soldiers did not fight naked but they were often carved like this to make them look more heroic.

Every four years a general truce was declared in Greece so people could travel safely to the Games at Olympia. This was necessary because there was always a war going on somewhere between one city-state and another. These wars usually started when a city-state needed more corn or goats.

Summer was the season for war and a typical war between cities started like this. A herald was sent out to declare war. Then an animal was sacrificed and the soothsayer studied its entrails to see if the gods were feeling helpful. If so, it was a good time to begin and the soldiers marched out to war. If not, they waited for a better day. Sometimes wars between small city-states only lasted one day, and the soldiers went home again at night.

The Greeks had no machines which could break down city walls if the people decided to take shelter and not fight. But because wars were fought during the summer, the corn was ripening. To lose a harvest was very serious, so a city might decide to fight rather than risk having its fields burned.

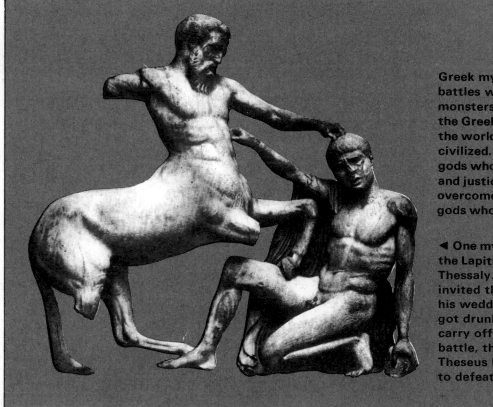

Greek myths are full of battles with fabulous monsters. This is the way the Greeks explained how the world became civilized. The Olympic gods who brought reason and justice had first to overcome the primitive gods who made the world.

◄ One myth was about the Lapiths who lived in Thessaly. Their king invited the centaurs to his wedding. The centaurs got drunk and tried to carry off the bride. In the battle, the Greek hero Theseus helped the king to defeat the centaurs.

◄ These reliefs show some of the stages in a war between city-states.

Ranks of *hoplites* march into the enemy's land, cutting down fruit-trees, trampling crops and even digging up garlic roots as they go. The opposing army waits for them, lined up outside the city walls.

Safe inside the city walls with their animals, the women watch. The two lines march at each other, singing battle hymns to Apollo. They meet with a clash of shields, push until one line breaks, then fight hand-to-hand until one side runs away.

The city might decide not to fight a pitched battle. Then the soldiers will have to try to scale the walls under the hail of rocks. Or they might settle down to starve the city, or else simply destroy the crops and go home.

If there is a battle and one side runs away, the victors set up a pyramid of captured shields. They wait until the losers admit defeat by asking permission to carry away their dead. On the left, a city surrenders. The seated man is making terms with the victorious Greek commander.

# A great festival

A model of the Athens *acropolis* and the procession for the festival of Athena. Treasure was kept in the temples and people prayed by the open air altar.

Statue of Athena

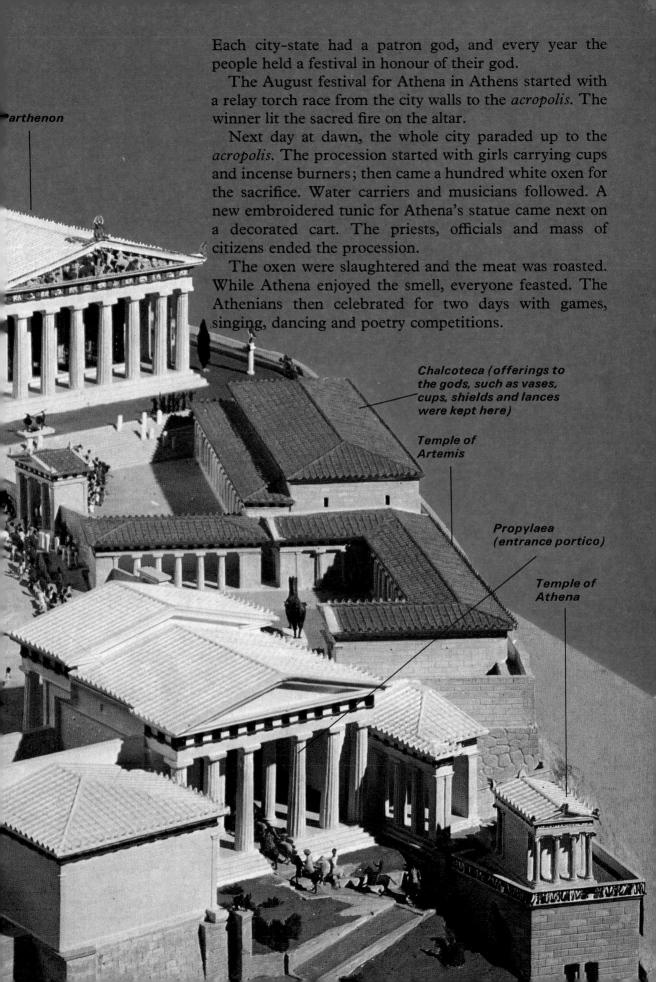

Each city-state had a patron god, and every year the people held a festival in honour of their god.

The August festival for Athena in Athens started with a relay torch race from the city walls to the *acropolis*. The winner lit the sacred fire on the altar.

Next day at dawn, the whole city paraded up to the *acropolis*. The procession started with girls carrying cups and incense burners; then came a hundred white oxen for the sacrifice. Water carriers and musicians followed. A new embroidered tunic for Athena's statue came next on a decorated cart. The priests, officials and mass of citizens ended the procession.

The oxen were slaughtered and the meat was roasted. While Athena enjoyed the smell, everyone feasted. The Athenians then celebrated for two days with games, singing, dancing and poetry competitions.

Parthenon

Chalcoteca (offerings to the gods, such as vases, cups, shields and lances were kept here)

Temple of Artemis

Propylaea (entrance portico)

Temple of Athena

# Apollo speaks

At Delphi, the god Apollo spoke directly to men through his priestess, the Pythia. Kings and statesmen came from all over the world to sacrifice a goat outside Apollo's temple and ask his advice. Only the priests were allowed to approach the Pythia who sat in a trance behind a veil in the temple.

Apollo's answers could sometimes be taken two ways. King Croesus of Lydia once asked if he should go to war with the Persians. Apollo said that if he did, an empire would be lost. Croesus thought that Apollo meant the Persian empire, but it was his own that was lost.

▼ The Pythia sits beside the stone *omphalos*, navel of the world. A priest passes on her words to the man who is consulting the oracle.

◄ The remains of Apollo's temple at Delphi. As god of colonists, he advised people where to found new cities.

*Cupping bowl for blood*

*Saw for amputations*

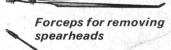

*Forceps for removing spearheads*

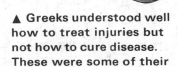

*Ointment spoon*

▲ Greeks understood well how to treat injuries but not how to cure disease. These were some of their medical instruments.

► A sick man sleeps in the temple. The god Asclepius appears to him in a dream to tell him how to cure his illness.

People often visited temples when they were ill because they hoped the gods would cure them. The shrines of Asclepius, the god of healing, were especially popular. And the bathing, rest, massage and simple food organized by the priests often did cure people.

As well as going to a temple, a Greek might also visit a doctor. There were several schools of medicine and each had its own theory. The students of Hippocrates, the most famous ancient Greek doctor, believed that with rest and plain food, the body could cure itself.

# The Olympics

The *Pentathlon*

*A foot race.* The longest race was two *stade* (360 m.). There was no marathon.

*Discus throwing.* The discus was a flat, circular bronze plate.

*Long jump.* Athletes jumped from a standing position.

*Javelin throwing.* The javelin was used for hunting and in war.

*Wrestling.* No holds were barred.

**A discus thrower**

One of the great religious festivals in Greece was the games competition in honour of Zeus. Every four years a truce on war was declared, so that people from all over Greece could travel safely to Olympus.

Our modern Olympic Games are copied from this festival. In the opening ceremony now, an athlete lights the Olympic flame and the athletes swear to compete fairly. This is because in 776 BC an athlete first lit the fire on the altar where a sacrifice to Zeus was made.

There are no valuable prizes now because there were none then. Athletes competed in honour of Zeus, not for money. A winner won great glory, but his prize was only a simple wreath of wild olive leaves.

▲ The starting line for the races at the stadium at Delphi.

▼ Stadium entrance at Olympia. The stadium was one *stade* long.

▲ Athlete's oil jar and *strigil*. He raced naked and afterwards he oiled his dusty skin and scraped it clean with a *strigil*.

▲ Long jumpers held metal or stone weights. We do not know if they kept hold of them or threw them behind as they jumped.

Statues, such as the one on the opposite page, show us how much the Greeks admired beauty of form and proportion in art. What they admired most in men was *arete*, which means excellence in everything.

This is why the *pentathlon* was the main event at the Olympic Games. The *pentathlon* included five different sports and an athlete had to compete in them all.

There were no professional sportsmen, for no one admired a specialist, however good he was. The athletes were ordinary citizens. They spent part of their day exercising and practising different sports at the gymnasium. This was because they thought that a fit, healthy body was as important as a well-educated mind.

# Going to school

Athenian law said that every boy must learn a trade but there was no law about school. Schools were private and not everyone could afford the fees. There were no girls' schools: they had to learn at home.

If he went to school, a boy learned to read, write, count with an abacus, play the lyre, sing, dance and recite poetry. It was important to be able to recite well, for poetry was meant to be heard not read. He spent the afternoons exercising in the gymnasium.

Boys chanted poetry to the lyre.

A master listens to a boy reading.

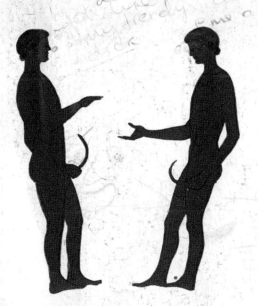

Boys spent half the day in the gymnasium.

A master corrects a boy's wax tablet.

At 15, an Athenian boy left school. He became apprenticed, perhaps to a potter, a stonemason or a doctor. If he wanted to study further, he had to find a teacher himself, for there were no universities. But he might find a philosopher who taught groups of young men outside in the *agora* or in the gymnasium.

Education in Sparta was very different. Physical fitness was more important than anything else. In their state boarding schools, the boys learnt to endure cold, hunger and pain. They learnt discipline and instant obedience. They became perfect soldiers and some of the best dancers in Greece. But they did not learn poetry, reading, writing or arithmetic.

▼ A scene from the *Odyssey*. To stop the sirens' singing from luring them onto the rocks, the crew stuff their ears with wax and tie Odysseus to the mast.

Homer's poetry was the most important subject in Greek education. Homer wrote two long poems. The *Iliad* is the story of the Trojan War. The *Odyssey* describes the adventures of Odysseus on his way home from the War. These poems provided religious education, history, geography and literature. Schoolboys recited the poems at festivals. The Greeks thought that men became better by hearing stories of the gods and heroes.

# A day at the theatre

▼ The main actors acted on the *proskenion* roof in masks and platform shoes, so that they could be seen from the back row. The chorus danced and sang on the orchestra.

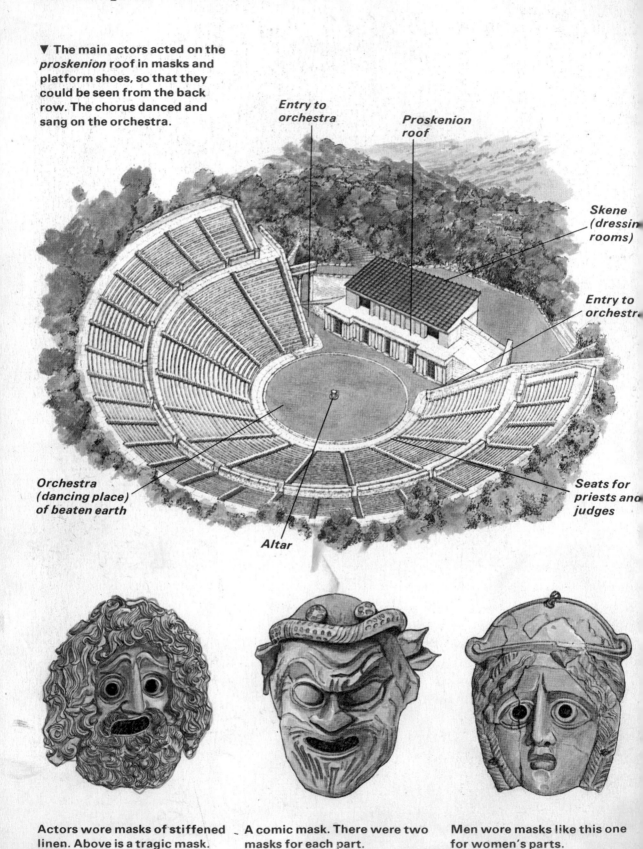

Entry to orchestra

Proskenion roof

Skene (dressing rooms)

Entry to orchestra

Seats for priests and judges

Orchestra (dancing place) of beaten earth

Altar

Actors wore masks of stiffened linen. Above is a tragic mask.

A comic mask. There were two masks for each part.

Men wore masks like this one for women's parts.

One of the great events of the year for a Greek was a visit to the theatre. Plays were only put on for ten days in the year. Each play was only performed once and naturally everyone wanted to see it, so the theatre had to be huge.

People went to the theatre soon after sunrise. They paid their two *obols* (a third of a *drachma*) to get in. If anyone was too poor to pay, the state paid for him out of a special fund for festivals.

Once in the theatre, people sat there all day. They took food with them to eat in the short intervals between the plays. They watched three tragedies or three comedies followed by a short satyr farce. The audience usually knew the plot, for plays were almost always based on well-known myths or legends. The interesting thing was to see what the poet had done with the story.

The greatest difference between Greek theatre and the modern theatre was that Greek plays were part of a religious festival held in honour of the gods. For the theatre had begun as a festival of songs which told stories of the gods. Then one man stepped out of the line of singers to act the part of the main character. Later a second actor was introduced, and gradually plays as we know them developed.

▲ Greeks today still flock to the ancient Greek theatre at Epidaurus to see the plays of the famous ancient Greek poets.

▲ Judges sat in these seats at the front and awarded prizes for the best plays each year.

# The Gods of Olympus

Far back in history, there had been many local gods. Each was linked with a sacred place such as a mysterious corner of a forest or a quiet pool. Gradually, twelve gods became more important than the rest. In 750 BC Hesiod wrote the history of these twelve gods of Mount Olympus. Each god had his or her own special sign or symbol.

**Zeus** the all-wise ruled the gods on Olympus and protected Greece. He sent the rain, wind and dew and was master of the thunder. His special symbols were the oak tree and eagle. The Olympic Games were held in his honour.

**Hera** was Zeus's third wife. She protected wives and mothers. Her own marriage was not always happy, for Zeus kept falling in love with other women. Her symbols were the pomegranate and the peacock.

**Athena,** daughter of Zeus and his first wife, Metis, was the goddess of wisdom. She protected heroes and craftsmen, taught men to tame horses and invented the potter's wheel. Her symbols were the owl and the olive tree.

**Apollo,** son of Zeus and Leto, was the god of light, music, healing and sudden death. At Delphi he gave advice to men. He protected farmers, colonists and musicians. His symbols were the lyre and laurel tree.

**Artemis,** twin-sister of Apollo, spent her time hunting deer. Like Apollo, she was a goddess of light and her arrows brought sudden death. She protected girls and virgins. Her symbols were the bear and the bow.

**Hermes,** son of Zeus and Maia, was the messenger of the gods. He invented the lyre, boxing and racing. He protected traders and travellers and led the dead to the underworld. His symbol was a winged staff.

**Ares,** son of Zeus and Hera, was hated by all the gods. He was the god of war, not heroic battle that Athena loved, but blind, brutal destruction. He went to war accompanied by his two sons, Fear and Fright.

**Hephaestus,** son of Zeus and Hera, was the lame blacksmith of the gods. He first taught men how to use fire to work metal, and was the protector of blacksmiths. His symbols were the hammer and tongs.

**Aphrodite,** a cousin of Zeus, was the most beautiful of the goddesses. The jealous Hera made her marry Hephaestus, but they were never happy. As goddess of love, she protected all kinds of lovers. She was also the goddess of gardens.

**Poseidon** lost a battle with his brother Zeus for control of the sky and moved to a palace under the Aegean Sea. He ruled the seas and rivers. All sailors sacrificed to him. With a stroke of his trident he caused earthquakes and storms.

**Hestia,** older sister of Zeus, was the most loved of all. She was the calm goddess of the household fire and the public hearth which burned constantly in the town hall of every city. She protected the city, the home and the family.

**Demeter,** sister of Zeus, was goddess of the fruitful earth. She taught men to grow corn. Every year, her daughter spent six months with Hades in the underworld. Demeter's sorrow over this caused the winter.

Apollo

Art...

Ares

He:

Hera

Hephaestus

Zeus

Hermes

Athena

Poseidon

Demeter

Aphrodite

# Lesser Gods

**Hades**, the brother of Zeus, ruled the underworld in the centre of the earth. It was a kind of limbo where the dead wandered as pale shadows.

**Eos**, in her purple robe, tipped dew over the world each morning. Then her brother **Helios** rose into the sky in his golden sun-chariot.

**Selene** drove her silver moon-chariot drawn by two horses across the sky at night. She was worshipped on the days of the new and full moon.

**Pan** was the god of the woods and pastures. He had the horns, legs and ears of a goat. He invented the pan-pipes and protected shepherds and their flocks.

**Dionysus**, son of Zeus and a mortal woman, was the god of wine. He travelled the world, bringing the gift of wine to men. The drama festivals were held in his honour.

**Asclepius**, son of Apollo, was the god of healing. When he used his art to revive the dead, Hades complained to Zeus. Asclepius was struck dead for defying nature's laws.

**Themis**, second wife of Zeus, organized the ceremonies on Mount Olympus. On earth she was the goddess of justice. In her scales she weighed the innocent and guilty.

**The three Fates**, shadowy daughters of Night, arrived at a man's birth. They were the destiny that no man could escape. Together they spun and cut the thread of life.

51

**2000BC** Wandering tribes from Western Russia settle in Greece and mix with the people there. The Greek language develops from this mixture. From 1600 to 1200 BC the Mycenean civilization develops. Kings rule from great stone palaces and eat from gold plate. Court officials keep accounts and send trading ships all over the Mediterranean.

**1200BC** Traditional date of the siege of Troy. After ten years of war, the Greeks get inside the city walls by hiding in a wooden horse. The unsuspecting Trojans drag it into the city and are surprised and defeated by the Greeks who jump out.

▲ **Warlike tribes pass through Greece destroying palaces**

During the next 200 years, warlike tribes from the north invade the Mediterranean. They pass through Greece, destroying palaces as they go. With their trade routes cut by pirates, the Mycenean kings cannot keep up their rich way of life. They begin to fight each other. The kingdoms collapse, the people return to farming and even the art of writing is lost.

Some of the invaders, the Dorians, settle in Greece among the original inhabitants, the Ionians. But in Laconia, the tribe called Spartans turn the Ionians into state slaves. Some Ionians flee to the coast of Asia and found Greek settlements there. This period is called the Dark Ages because we know very little about it.

**850BC** Traditional date of Homer. Greece slowly comes out of the Dark Ages. City-states begin to form as people move from their villages to live around the central fort, the *polis*. Aristocrats rule the cities.

A new kind of warfare develops using close ranks of heavily-armed soldiers called *hoplites*. The Greeks borrow Phoenician letters and add vowels, making the Greek alphabet. The first Olympic Games are held in 776 BC.

As trade increases and the population grows, many people become poorer and are forced to sell their land. Some emigrate to find new land, others call for changes. Sparta solves her problem by taking over her neighbour, Messenia, and turning the people into state slaves called *helots*.

▲ **People emigrate to find new land**

**650BC** In some states people revolt against their aristocratic rulers. They support tyrants who promise them a share in land and government. In other states, a chief magistrate is elected to sort out the problems. For the first time, codes of laws are drawn up to govern the states. The Messenian *helots* revolt against Sparta. She makes new laws that turn all Spartans into full-time soldiers in case of another revolt.

**594BC** Solon is appointed chief magistrate of Athens. He begins the move towards democracy by allowing all citizens to vote in the assembly and setting up juries to try law cases. Over the next century the assembly becomes the most powerful part of the government and all citizens become eligible for all government jobs.

The Athenians build a navy with the profits from a silver mine discovered in 483 BC. Sparta forms a military alliance with other states in southern Greece.

**499BC** The Greek cities in Asia Minor, helped by Athens, revolt against their Persian overlord. The revolt fails and Persia sends an army to punish Athens. Helped by the city of Plataea, the Athenians defeat the Persians on the plain of Marathon in 490 BC.

**480BC** Xerxes, king of Persia, sends a huge army to invade Greece. The states form an alliance. 300 Spartans hold the Pass of

▲ 300 Spartans hold the Pass of Thermopylae against the Persian army

▲ Sparta invades Athenian territory

Thermopylae for two days against the whole Persian army, giving time for Athens to be evacuated. The Persians enter and burn Athens. But in the Bay of Salamis, the Greek navy destroys the Persian fleet.

Over the next 50 years of peace, Athenians produce their greatest art and poetry. At the same time Athens becomes more powerful. She forms a league of friendly states each of whom pay her every year for the upkeep of the navy. Then she turns the league into an empire. She punishes the states if they try to leave it. Some turn to Sparta for help.

**431BC** War breaks out between Athens and Sparta. But because Sparta has mainly land forces and Athens mainly sea power, they cannot get to grips. The war drags on. Sparta invades Athenian territory year after year. At last Sparta, with Persia's help, cuts Athens' corn supply by blocking her sea routes. Athens surrenders. Sparta tries to rule all Greece, but city-states keep revolting.

**350BC** As Sparta becomes weaker, Philip of Macedon enters Greece. He organizes the whole country into a federation under his leadership. He dies a year later, leaving Greece to his son, Alexander the Great.

Greek philosophers asked questions such as: what is the world made of?

In trying to answer these questions, they began to study the world and the relationships between shapes, between animals and between numbers. These studies were the beginning of modern science, algebra, geometry, zoology, botany, geology and history.

Greek writers and artists studied relationships too. Playwrights wrote about the relationship of man and the gods. Artists studied the relationship between the different parts of the body, in order to create perfect beauty.

▲ A statue of the playwright, Sophocles.

## φιλοσοφια
## philosophy

**Thales** (636-546 BC) was a philosopher and astrologer who thought that the universe was made of water.

**Pythagoras** (582-546 BC) set up a secret community in Italy where people studied. He and his followers were interested in mathematics, geometry and music.

**Democritus** (460-370 BC) developed the theory that the world was made of an infinite number of tiny atoms.

**Socrates** (469-399 BC) got people to question their religious beliefs. This was thought to be dangerous, so he was forced to kill himself by drinking hemlock.

**Plato** (428-348 BC) wrote important books on religion and philosophy which are still read today. Some of his ideas are found in religions such as Christianity.

**Aristotle** (384-322 BC) was Plato's pupil. He made a great contribution to many fields of knowledge, including philosophy, physics, biology and zoology.

## θεατρον
## theatre

**Aeschylus** (525-456 BC) introduced the second actor into drama. Until now, there had only been a chorus of singers and one actor. His plays, the *Oresteia*, tell how justice came to Athens.

**Sophocles** (496-407 BC). His most famous play is *Oedipus*, the story of the king who, by a cruel mistake, married his own mother.

**Euripides** (485-406 BC). In plays such as *Hippolytus*, he made his characters more like real people than characters had been before.

**Aristophanes** (450-385 BC) wrote his comedies all through the wars with

Sparta, helping people to relax and laugh.

# ιστορια
## history

**Herodotus** (484-425 BC) wrote the *Historiai* which means "enquiries". In these he tried for the first time to sort out fact from legend.

**Thucydides** (471-400 BC) wrote a long history of the war between Athens and Sparta.

**Xenophon** (431-354 BC) wrote several books about Socrates as well as finishing Thucydides' war history.

# ποιητης
## poet

**Homer** (ninth century BC) was the first and greatest of Greek poets. His two poems the *Iliad* and the *Odyssey* were the basis of Greek education.

**Hesiod** (eighth century BC) was a farmer-poet. He wrote a history of the gods and a poem of advice on farming.

**Sappho** (610-565 BC) was a lyric poetess. She ran a school for women poets.

**Pindar** (518-446 BC) was most famous for the odes he wrote for the banquets of the Olympic Games winners.

# τεχνη
## art

The Greek word *techne* means art or way of doing something. Many English words come from it.

**Duris** (around 580 BC). We know nothing about him apart from his wonderfully-painted red-figure pots.

**Pheidias** (460-429 BC) was the architect of the Parthenon (the large temple on the *acropolis* in Athens).

**Praxiteles** (around 350 BC). His fame was founded on his statues of Aphrodite.

# The Greek Alphabet

Many words which are used today come from the ancient Greek words. You can see this by looking at the Greek alphabet below and then at the Greek words with their English meanings on the left.

| Capital letter | Small letter | Name of the letter | Sound of the letter |
|---|---|---|---|
| Α | α | alpha | a (either as in *pat* or as in *part*) |
| Β | β | beta | b |
| Γ | γ | gamma | g (hard as in *got*) |
| Δ | δ | delta | d |
| Ε | ε | epsilon | e (as in *red*) |
| Ζ | ζ | zeta | z |
| Η | η | eta | e (like the *a* in *hay*) |
| Θ | θ | theta | th (as in *thin*) |
| Ι | ι | iota | i |
| Κ | κ | kappa | k |
| Λ | λ | lambda | l |
| Μ | μ | mu | m |
| Ν | ν | nu | n |
| Ξ | ξ | xi | x (like the *ks* sound in *axe*) |
| Ο | ο | omicron | o (as in *lot*) |
| Π | π | pi | p |
| Ρ | ρ | rho | rh, r |
| Σ | σ ς | sigma | s |
| Τ | τ | tau | t |
| Υ | υ | upsilon | u (either as *oo* in *look* or as *u* in *Hugh*) |
| Φ | φ | phi | ph |
| Χ | χ | chi | kh |
| Ψ | ψ | psi | ps |
| Ω | ω | omega | o (as in *home*) |

If ῾ is written over a letter it means that the letter is pronounced with an *h*.
e.g. ἥρως = hero.

If ᾿ is written over a letter it means there is no *h* sound.
e.g. ἔρως = Eros.

When sigma is at the end of a word it is written ς not σ.

# Ancient Greece

MACEDONIA

THRACE

• Amphipolis •

• Opella

CHALCIDICE

SAMOTHRACE

CHERSO
Sest

• Olynthus
• Potidaea

▲ Mount Athos

▲ Mount
Olympus

THESSALY

AEGEAN SEA

LES

Thermopylae •

Delphi •

EUBOEA
Chalcis •

• Eretria

CHIOS

Thebes •

ITHACA

• Marathon
Megara •      • Athens

CEPHALLENIA      Patrae •

• Piraeus

ANDROS

• Elis      Corinth •

ZYCANTHUS

• Olympia

Mycenae •

TENOS

IC

Argos •      Epidaurus •

MYCONOS

Tiryns •      • Troezen

DELOS

PAROS      NAXOS

• Sparta

MELOS

THERA

CRETE      • Cnossus

MEDITERRANEAN   SEA

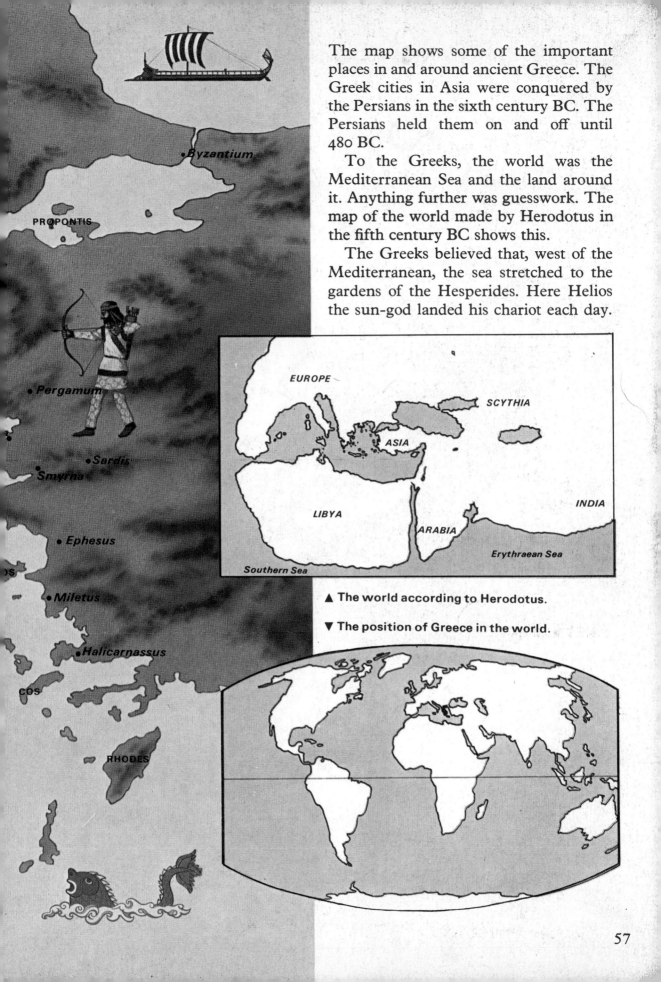

The map shows some of the important places in and around ancient Greece. The Greek cities in Asia were conquered by the Persians in the sixth century BC. The Persians held them on and off until 480 BC.

To the Greeks, the world was the Mediterranean Sea and the land around it. Anything further was guesswork. The map of the world made by Herodotus in the fifth century BC shows this.

The Greeks believed that, west of the Mediterranean, the sea stretched to the gardens of the Hesperides. Here Helios the sun-god landed his chariot each day.

▲ The world according to Herodotus.

▼ The position of Greece in the world.

# World history 1500 BC to 1 AD

|  | Greece | Europe | Asia |
|---|---|---|---|
| **1500 BC** | In small kingdoms on the Greek mainland, the Mycenean civilization develops after the destruction of the Minoan civilization on Crete. The Mycenean kings trade all over the Mediterranean. Warrior tribes from the North begin to invade the Mediterranean. | Central Italy is occupied from 2000 BC by a tribe from southern Russia, whose descendants were the Romans. The first invasion of Celts, chased west by Germanic tribes, settle in Switzerland and eastern France. | The Aryans, a cattle-raising agricultural people who worship nature gods, invade north India. They set up an empire in the Ganges basin. In China, under the Shang dynasty, the first astronomical observations are made. The pictographic script is developed. |
| **1200 BC** | The Mycenean civilization collapses. The Dorians invade Greece. Some Greeks flee to the coast of Asia. People live as subsistence farmers in small villages ruled by tribal chiefs. | Second wave of Celtic invaders settle in France and Spain and cross the channel to south-east England. The druids are their priests, teachers and judges. | The Aryan culture spreads to southern India. To control the people, the Aryans set up a system of four castes with priests or brahmins at the top. In China, under the western Chou dynasty, government and religion are controlled by the king. Only aristocrats are allowed to own land. |
| **900 BC** | Villagers move to central walled towns. The alphabet is invented. Overcrowded cities send out colonists. Trade increases. Tyrants, supported by the people, overthrow aristocrats and give the people more share in governing. | The Etruscans enter Italy and settle in the north and centre. 735 BC is the traditional date of the foundation of Rome. For a short time, the Etruscans take over power in Rome. Greece founds colonies in France, Sicily and Spain. | In India, the doctrine of reincarnation develops. The eastern Chou dynasty in China gains control over the surrounding states. China becomes divided into a loose federation of seven great states. |
| **600 BC** | City-states set up democratic or oligarchic governments. The states form an alliance and defeat the invading Persian army. Athens and Sparta become more powerful. War breaks out between them. Philip of Macedon takes control, forming Greece into a federation. His son Alexander succeeds him. | More Celts invade Britain. They trade in iron, lead and tin with the Phoenicians. In Rome there is a revolt against the Etruscans and a republic is set up. Rome gains control over central Italy and makes alliances with other parts of Italy. | Siddhartha Buddha is born and begins teaching in 519. The earliest surviving Sanskrit grammar is written. In China, Confucius is born. The seven great states fight until Ch'in conquers its rivals. Alexander reaches India, but his soldiers make him turn back. |
| **300 BC** <br> **1 AD** | After Alexander's death, his generals fight one another for control of his empire and divide it between them. Many Greeks emigrate to Near Eastern cities. Greece becomes a Roman province. Many Greeks are taken to Italy as slaves. | Rome defeats Carthage. She gains control of Sicily and turns Spain into a Roman province. She helps Greece against Macedonia and turns Greece into a Roman province. Romans land in Britain. The Roman republic collapses. Augustus becomes the first emperor. | Buddhist king Asoka Maurya unites India, but is overthrown by the Brahmin Sunga dynasty. The golden age of philosophy in China, influenced by Greek thought. The Great Wall is started and the sundial invented. By conquest, China achieves its modern frontiers. |

| Africa | Near East | America |
|---|---|---|
| | | |

**1500 BC**

| | | |
|---|---|---|
| Egypt wins back lower Egypt from Nubian tribes. Under Tutmosis, Egypt goes on to conquer a great empire as far as the Euphrates River (in modern Iraq). The Children of Israel, under Moses, leave Egypt. | The Hittites, a nomad tribe from central Asia, invade Turkey and Anatolia. They borrow cuneiform writing from the Sumerians. Their cities are run by court officials. They develop a complex legal system. They conquer Syria from the Hurrians. | The Maya people migrate from the north and settle in what are now British Honduras, Guatemala and Yucatan. Small farming communities spring up, using flint tools and trading with each other. |

**1200 BC**

| | | |
|---|---|---|
| Egypt loses its empire to the same warrior tribes who invade Greece. Egypt is split, with the High priest ruling in Thebes and the king in Tanis. Shosqueng reunites Egypt, invades Palestine and robs the temple in Jerusalem. | The Hittite empire is invaded and destroyed by warrior tribes from the north. The space left is filled by Phrygians from the east and Semites from Arabia. The Israelites reach Palestine. | On the west coast of South America small cultures develop. Stone-age farmers grow maize and manioc, build stone houses and weave cloth. They were mostly wiped out by the Incas in 400 AD. |

**900 BC**

| | | |
|---|---|---|
| The Nok culture develops in central Nigeria. The farmers use stone tools and make terracotta pottery.<br>The Kushites from the Upper Nile valley conquer Egypt. | Palestine splits into Judah and Israel. Judah asks the Assyrians to help them conquer Israel. The Assyrians conquer both, as well as the coastal cities of Egypt and Phoenicia. The Medes and Babylonians join to split the Assyrian empire. Persia, vassal state of the Medes, begins to grow. | The Olmec civilization develops in Mexico. The Olmecs invent the calendar and know how to write. Their game, Tlachtli, a form of basketball, spreads through central America. |

**600 BC**

| | | |
|---|---|---|
| The Assyrians conquer lower Egypt, pushing the Kushites back into Africa. The Kushites learn from the Assyrians how to smelt iron. They settle in the city of Meroe where they develop a huge iron industry, becoming very rich. | The Babylonians conquer Jerusalem but are themselves conquered by Cyrus, King of Persia. The Persian empire spreads over the Near East. The Persians invade Greece but are defeated. Alexander the Great of Macedonia conquers the Persian empire and spreads his empire to India. | Olmec culture begins to decline. Their city, Monte Alban, is taken over by the Mayas. For the first time, they begin to make coloured pottery painted with realistic human figures.<br>Inca people called the Paracas and Nazcas appear in Peru. |

**300 BC**

| | | |
|---|---|---|
| Rome conquers Egypt. Kushite trade extends to Arabia and India. The Nigerians learn to work iron. Bantu people from the borders of Nigeria gradually spread over eastern and southern Africa, by using the Congo river system. | After Alexander's death, the Near East is ruled by two of his generals. Greek culture spreads through the area as Greeks take over all government jobs. Rome conquers the area, turning the states into Roman provinces. | The Toltecs settle in the central plateau of Mexico. They build their great city of Teotihuacan, 13 km. (eight miles) square. |

**1 AD**

# Glossary

*acropolis* the fortress on the hill around which villagers settle to make the first towns.

*agora* the open space in the town centre where markets and public meetings were held.

**archaeologist** someone who studies historical remains.

*archon* an official who ran festivals and administered laws.

**assembly** the meeting of all citizens to discuss and vote on how to run their city-state.

*chiton* a Greek tunic.

**citizen** only citizens took part in government or were allowed to own land in the city-state. A person could not be a citizen of Athens unless both his parents were citizens.

**city-state** a town and the farmland around it.

*Dorian* warlike Greeks from the north-west who invaded Greece in the twelfth century BC. The Spartans were Dorians.

**gymnasium** at first an exercise ground. Later it became the place where philosophers held their open-air schools.

*helots* the state slaves who worked the farms for the Spartans.

*hoplites* heavily-armed foot-soldiers.

*Ionians* the people who were living in Greece when the Dorians invaded.

*krater* a type of large vase.

*oligarchy* a system of government in which a state is ruled by only a few people.

*perioeci* means "dwellers around". They lived in villages around the plain of Sparta and were governed by the Spartans.

*polis* at first meant the same as *acropolis*. In the fifth century BC it meant the whole city-state.

**relief** a carving on which the figures or objects are slightly raised from a flat surface.

*silphium* a vegetable, considered very valuable by the Greeks, but now extinct.

*strigil* an instrument for scraping the skin after exercise or bathing.

# Index